POISONERS AND PRETENDERS

BY MICHAEL CHINERY

CHERRYTREE BOOKS

A Cherrytree Book

Designed and produced by
A S Publishing

First published 2000
by Cherrytree Press
327 High Street
Slough
Berkshire
SL1 1TX

British Library Cataloguing in Publication Data

Chinery, Michael
Poisoners and Pretenders. — (Secrets of the rainforest)
1.Poisonous animals — Juvenile literature
2.Poisonous plants — Juvenile literature
3.Rain forest animals — Juvenile literature
4.Rain forest plants — Juvenile literature
I.Title
591.6'5

ISBN 1842 34002 6

Design: Richard Rowan
Artwork: Malcolm Porter
Consultant: Sue Fogden

Printed in Hong Kong by Wing King Tong Co. Ltd

Acknowledgements
Photographs: *All by courtesy of Michael & Patricia Fogden*

❂ CONTENTS ❂

❂ POISONERS AND PRETENDERS ❂

RAINFORESTS grow in wet parts of the world, particularly in the tropics around the equator where it is hot all year round and it rains almost every day. More plants and animals live in the rainforests than anywhere else on earth. Many of them have remarkable ways of defending themselves against their enemies, using poison and all manner of tricks. Some, including wasps, spiders and many snakes, also use poison to capture their prey. Some get their poisons from the plants they eat; others manufacture it inside their bodies.

With so many fierce animals ready to kill them, many smaller animals evade their enemies by staying still and appearing to merge with their background. This kind of camouflage also protects larger animals. Still other animals pretend to be fiercer than they are or gain protection by being mistaken for more dangerous creatures.

THERE are thousands of different poisonous creatures in the rainforests, like this spider which has sunk its fangs into a katydid. But very few of them are really dangerous to people, so you can walk through a rainforest without undue fear. Many rainforest plants are also poisonous, but a lot of the poisons they contain are useful as medicines when used in small doses. Rainforest peoples have known about these medicines for a very long time. Curare, from the bark of a South American tree, is important in surgical operations. It relaxes the patient's muscles and allows the surgeon to work properly. Many other precious substances probably lie undiscovered in the rainforests and that is one reason why we must look after the forests.

▲ Few creatures attack bumblebees because of their stings, but this is not a bee: it is a moth pretending to be a bee.

◄ Looking like part of the plant, this katydid, a kind of bush-cricket, fools passing predators.

▼ This monster is another katydid. It frightens away predators by looking far fiercer than it is.

POISONOUS OR VENOMOUS

Many poisonous species have their harmful substances spread throughout their bodies. These animals taste nasty and may be dangerous to eat, but they do not attack other creatures. Their poisons are used purely for defence. Other creatures store their poisons in particular parts of their bodies. These poisons are called venoms and the animals usually have stings or other weapons for injecting the venom into their victims. Animals with poisonous weapons are known as venomous creatures, to distinguish them from those that are simply poisonous to eat.

Some animal venoms are simple acids that sting or burn where they enter the body, but their effect is local and soon wears off. Many ants deter their attackers by spraying them with formic acid. Most animal venoms are, however, more complex. Some affect the victim's nervous system, hindering breathing or disrupting the blood circulation by interfering with the control of the heart. Other venoms destroy blood cells or cause the blood to solidify in the veins and arteries, and yet others digest and destroy the tissues around the site of the wound.

☀ DANGER BEWARE! ☀

HAVING A poisonous body or a disgusting taste is a good form of defence, but even the strongest poison is useless if an animal has to be bitten and killed or injured before a predator discovers that it does not taste very nice. Most animals that rely on unpleasant tastes for protection have ways of advertising the fact. They have bright colours or bold patterns that are known as warning coloration. Black and yellow are common warning colours, but black and red or black and white are equally effective. Some creatures employ more elaborate colour schemes, but the important thing is that they are eye-catching and memorable.

EAT ME IF YOU DARE

Experiments show that young, inexperienced creatures try almost anything they find, but spit out distasteful things straight away. They soon learn to associate bold colour patterns with foul tastes or stings, and after that they leave the distasteful animals alone. Although some prey animals have to die before the predators have learned their lessons, the warning colours do benefit the prey species as a whole.

▲ Many animals protected by warning colours also have nasty smells. This moth exudes a foul-smelling poisonous foam when it is alarmed.

▶ The fire-bellied toad hides its brightest colours until danger threatens. Their sudden appearance deters predators.

NATURAL SELECTION

NATURAL selection is the force that guides evolution and ensures that living things are well suited, or adapted, to their surroundings. It works because individuals that are not well suited do not survive: they are caught and eaten or else die from disease or starvation. Animals with better camouflage or more poison survive to breed, and pass on their good qualities to the next generation. The process, repeated over and over, results in the protection getting better and better. The ancestors of this Amazonian caterpillar (right) probably had only mildly poisonous spines, but predators removed the least poisonous individuals in each generation and the insect gradually acquired the vicious spines it has today – as a result of natural selection.

Many insects with warning colours have tough skins that limit the damage when they are attacked. Some also have bodies that heal quickly after damage, so the number of animals that die before their predators learn to leave them alone is kept to a low level.

▼ Warning coloration works so well that insects like this moth often rest openly on plants and make no attempt to escape if disturbed.

HARMLESS MIMICS

You do not have to be poisonous to gain protection from your enemies. Many harmless rainforest species deceive their enemies simply by looking like poisonous species. Having learned the hard way to leave poisonous species alone, the predators also ignore all other creatures with similar colours or patterns. This kind of trickery is called mimicry. The poisonous species are known as models and the harmless tricksters as mimics.

Many bees and wasps are models and advertise their stings and unpleasant tastes with yellow and black warning colours. They are copied by many harmless mimics, including moths, beetles and flies – particularly hover-flies. Many edible butterflies also mimic poisonous species, especially in the tropical forests.

The poisonous models are generally more numerous than their mimics. This ensures that most birds and other predators meet more models than mimics, so they learn that the bold patterns are associated with unpleasant experiences. If the edible or harmless mimics were more common than the poisonous species, the predators would find that most of the boldly marked insects actually tasted good. The system would then not work because all the insects would be attacked and none of them would benefit.

MIMICRY RINGS
. . . .

THESE two butterflies look alike and they both taste nasty, but they are not closely related. They actually belong to two very different families. They form part of a mimicry ring, which may contain lots of poisonous insects with a similar colour or pattern. All the insects

in the ring benefit because, once a predator has learned to recognise the warning coloration, all the species sharing it are protected. Only a few members of each species are killed before the predators learn the lesson, and the more species there are in each ring the better, because fewer individuals of each will perish.

▲ The venomous coral snake (top) is a danger to other animals and they keep well away. It is the model for the harmless fire-bellied snake that mimics it.

HOW MIMICRY DEVELOPED

Mimics do not set out to copy their models. Mimicry, just like camouflage (see page 24), has evolved through the processes of natural selection. At one time, the similarities between the mimic and model would not have been very great, but even a slight resemblance to a poisonous model can help a mimic to escape by causing a predator to hesitate for a split second. Over many generations, the mimicry gradually improved and produced today's amazing similarities. Even experienced naturalists often have difficulty in distinguishing mimics from their models.

◀ Anyone might think this creature is a wasp, but actually it is a glasswing moth that gains protection by looking like a wasp.

CREEPY CATERPILLARS

SOME OF THE smallest creatures in the rainforest are the most poisonous. Because it is warm all year round, butterflies and moths, and many other creatures, breed all year. So there are always millions of butterfly eggs and caterpillars. Caterpillars are soft and juicy, the perfect food for birds and many other predators.

For protection against these enemies, many caterpillars have poisonous fluids in their bodies and bright warning colours. Some smell nasty as well. These caterpillars often live in clusters, making their colours and smells even more conspicuous. Predators keep well away from them. Many other caterpillars have real weapons that can inflict painful wounds if they are molested.

IRRITATING CATERPILLARS

Hairy or spiny coats make many caterpillars difficult or painful for predators to swallow. If they are attacked, the caterpillars may flick their bodies from side to side and try to drive the spines into the faces of their enemies. This can be very painful for monkeys and other small animals. Some spines and hairs are hollow and full of venom. Their pointed tips penetrate the skin and then snap off to release the stinging venom. All hairy caterpillars should be handled with care. The caterpillars of some South American silkmoths have venomous bristles that can cause severe bleeding even if you just brush your hand over them.

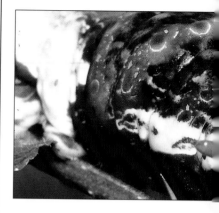

SWALLOWTAIL ATTACK

WHEN a swallowtail butterfly caterpillar is attacked, a forked sausage-like swelling called an osmeterium bursts out from behind its head. It is usually brightly coloured and its sudden appearance is enough to frighten small birds. Its acidic secretions may also

▼ This hairy tussock moth caterpillar may look pretty, but its hairs can cause severe skin irritation.

▶ To predators, these caterpillars, clustered together, must look even more alarming than they would singly.

irritate the birds' eyes and noses. The osmeterium also gives out a strong scent, with each swallowtail species having its own particular smell. This is often quite pleasant to human noses, but it probably repels insect enemies, including the ichneumons that lay their eggs on or inside the caterpillars.

Some caterpillars incorporate their hairs into the silken cocoons that they spin before turning into pupae. When large numbers of moths emerge from their cocoons at the same time they scatter millions of the poisonous hairs into the air as they fly, and sometimes cause widespread outbreaks of rashes and sore throats. Many tropical caterpillars surround their pupation sites with hairs as a protection against ants, which are major enemies of pupae in tropical areas.

FIRE BEASTS

SOME South American caterpillars are known as guinea pig caterpillars because their long, shaggy coats make them look like miniature guinea pigs. These caterpillars are very dangerous. The venomous spines hidden among their long hairs can cause severe headaches and serious damage to the skin, and some people need hospital treatment. The caterpillars are known as 'fire beasts' in some areas because their stings produce such a severe burning sensation.

SPIDERS, SCORPIONS AND CENTIPEDES

SPIDERS KILL their prey with venom produced in glands in the front part of the body. When the spider bites, the venom is pumped out through the fangs with great force. Spiders lurk everywhere in tropical forests. Huge webs, some a metre across, stretch from tree to tree and their silk is so strong that they do not always break when a person walks into them. Birds are often caught in the webs, but the spiders do not really want birds to fly into their webs and damage them, so many of them exhibit bold warning colours, especially red or yellow on a black background. Some web-spinning spiders also have long spines that prevent birds from swallowing them.

TARANTULAS

Not all rainforest spiders make webs. Many are hunters. The big bird-eating spiders, often called tarantulas, nest on the forest floor and come out at night to catch mice and lizards. Some of them climb the trees and drag young

▼ This spider looks like a colourful jewel and could well be mistaken for a flower bud.

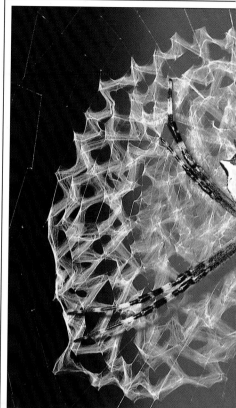

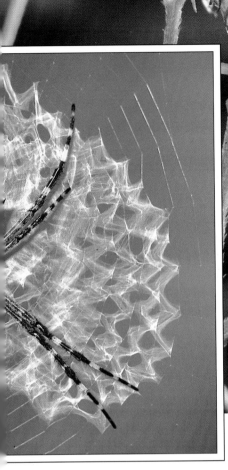

▲ Hidden in a cluster of flowers, this crab spider has caught a bumblebee.

▲ The thick white bands of silk in the middle of this web help to hide the spider from hungry birds.

birds from their nests. They have huge fangs, but they are not generally dangerous to people. Some of the smaller spiders are much more poisonous.

CRAB CAMOUFLAGE

Crab spiders sit motionless on plants or on the ground and seize any insect that comes within reach of their big front legs. They are usually so well camouflaged that their victims are unaware of the danger. Some crab spiders look just like bird droppings. This disguise protects them from birds and also helps them to obtain food. Butterflies and other insects often feed on bird droppings and other dung to get valuable salt. If they land on one of the bird-dropping spiders, it is usually the last thing they do.

◀ This hairy bird-eating spider, or tarantula, looks terrifying but its irritating hairs are more harmful to humans than its bite.

VENOMOUS CENTIPEDES

Centipedes are fast-running predators. Many species live in rainforests, on tree trunks and branches as well as on the ground. The biggest ones are about 30 cm long and they eat lizards, birds and small mammals as well as insects and spiders. Their weapons are a pair of venomous fangs that curve around the head. Venom is produced in the base of each fang and is forced out when the fangs strike. Centipede venom is deadly to most small animals, and a bite from one of the larger centipedes is quite painful to people. The venom can cause blisters and may destroy the flesh around the bites.

Some large tropical centipedes can nip painfully with their back legs as well as biting with their fangs. They can even catch prey with their back legs. Both ends are often brightly coloured to warn enemies to keep away. The centipedes can also secrete repellent fluids.

FOUL-TASTING MILLIPEDES

Millipedes are slow-moving herbivores. Most of them can secrete bitter-tasting fluids from glands on their sides. These fluids protect the millipedes from most predators, although toads are not put off by them. Large millipedes, up to 15 cm in length, can fire sprays or jets of fluid into the air. These poisons can give rise to painful blisters and can cause

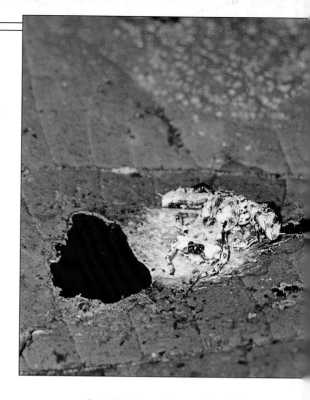

▲ Birds take no interest in their own droppings, so this spider's perfect disguise keeps it safe. If a butterfly comes to feed on the 'dropping', it will get a nasty shock.

▼ The lynx spider (left) is a hunter that runs down its prey. This pretty green specimen has caught a young plant bug.

STING IN THE TAIL

SCORPIONS are related to the spiders but instead of fangs they have a sting at the tip of the tail. Many live in rainforests, hiding away during the daytime and coming out to feed on insects and spiders at night. They also catch lizards and small rodents.

To inject its venom, the scorpion flicks its tail forward over its head at lightning speed and drives the sting into its victim. Muscles in the bulb contract and pump the venom into the wound. Scorpions use their stings mainly for protection, and sting their prey only if it struggles. This scorpion has used only its claws to catch its prey – a leaf-like katydid whose disguise has failed to protect it in this instance.

▼ This long-legged centipede (centre) is very fast and can easily catch spiders and beetles in the trees or on the ground.

▼ This giant millipede (right) feeds on dead leaves but its bright colours warn that it is still very poisonous.

blindness in any animal that tries to eat the millipedes. Some millipedes surround themselves with deadly cyanide gas when they are alarmed. The millipedes cannot store the poison in their bodies, so they make it in little pouches and fire it out immediately.

FEARSOME FROGS AND TOADS

FROGS LIVE at all levels in the rainforest, from the ground to the tops of the tallest trees. So much water is trapped in the vegetation that some kinds are able to live and breed in the tree-tops and never come down to the ground. Many of them have suckers on their toes that help them cling to the shiniest leaves. They are active by day and by night and they eat all sorts of insects, as well as spiders and worms.

SLIMY PROTECTION

All frogs are covered with a thin layer of slime that oozes from glands in the skin. It helps to keep the skin moist when the animals are out of water. Frogs breathe partly through their thin skins, but oxygen can pass through the skin only if it is moist. The slime of most frogs is also slightly poisonous and it kills most of the bacteria that might damage the thin skin. This is why frogs can live safely in dirty ponds. When a frog is frightened, it pumps out extra slime, making itself extra slippery so that it can escape more easily if it is caught by an enemy.

FROG OVERKILL

THERE are about 100 different kinds of arrow-poison frogs and most of them advertise their poisonous nature with really brilliant colours. The animals are protected mainly by the foul taste of their skin secretions, which may also cause a burning sensation in the mouth. Predators immediately let go of any frog they pick up, and then remember not to touch any more with the same colours. The frogs do not need such powerful poisons to defend themselves. It just happens that some of their secretions are unusually poisonous.

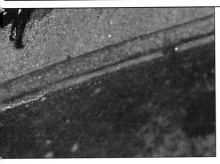

▲ The blue arrow-poison frog (right) and the kokoe-pa arrow-poison frog (left) are among the most poisonous animals in the world.

◄ The skin of this bright little tree frog is almost translucent. The poisonous slime on its skin keeps it moist and free from germs.

▶ The toad-eater snake specialises in eating toads, but it takes a brave snake to cope with a toad that has puffed itself up to twice its normal size.

ARROW-POISON FROGS

A frog's slime is not usually harmful to people, but a few species produce extremely poisonous slime that can kill people if it gets into their blood. The most poisonous of these frogs live in the rainforests of South and Central America. They are commonly known as arrow-poison frogs because the forest people collect the poison and use it on their hunting arrows. These weapons quickly kill any animal that they hit. Even a tiny scratch can cause death. The poisons affect the nerves and muscles and cause paralysis and heart failure. But they act only when they enter the blood through a wound. They are destroyed by digestive juices, so animals killed by the poisoned arrows can be eaten quite safely.

Some arrow-poison frogs are so poisonous that the hunters can pick up enough poison simply by rolling their arrows along the frogs' backs. Treated arrows remain poisonous for months.

❖ VENOMOUS SNAKES ❖

RAINFORESTS are full of snakes, though not all of them are poisonous. They kill their prey by injecting the venom through enlarged teeth called fangs. The venom is also used for defence when necessary. Some non-poisonous snakes can also inflict painful bites with their dagger-like teeth.

ON FLOOR AND BRANCH

Rainforest snakes live in the trees as well as among the dead leaves on the ground. Many of those that slither through the tall trees are slender snakes that resemble the lianas that twist and coil among the branches. They are difficult to see, so it is easy for them to creep up on or ambush their prey without being seen. The snakes have prehensile tails that wrap around the branches and prevent the animals from falling when they strike.

These tree-living snakes are active mainly in the daytime and most of them are ambushers. They strike at prey whenever it comes within range. They need good eyesight for picking out lizards and other small prey among the

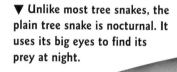

▼ Unlike most tree snakes, the plain tree snake is nocturnal. It uses its big eyes to find its prey at night.

▲ An eye-lash viper holds tight with its tail while striking at a passing hummingbird.

branches. Deep grooves in front of the eyes of the oriental whip snake allow it to see to the front as well as to each side. Several other slender, tree-living snakes have similar grooves.

▲ Coral snakes are the most colourful of the rainforest species. Although they have small fangs, they are very poisonous.

Ground-living snakes are mostly night-time hunters or ambushers. They lie in wait for their prey or track it down mainly by following its scent, but the pit vipers also home in on the warmth of their prey. Heat-sensitive pits on the snout detect very small changes in temperature and tell the snakes when warm-blooded prey is near. They can guide the snakes towards their prey as accurately as eyes, and the snakes can then strike with amazing accuracy even in the dark.

◀ Up to four metres long, the bushmaster is the largest and one of the most venomous snakes in South America. It is one of the pit vipers. Despite its size, its markings make it hard to see on the forest floor.

COME AND GET IT!

Some snakes actually lure their prey to their death by offering them some kind of 'bait'. Several species twitch their tails to attract birds. The African twig snake lures frogs and lizards by waving its orange tongue, which the prey may mistake for a juicy caterpillar. The twig snake is well camouflaged at rest, but when it spots a frog or a lizard prey it sticks out its colourful tongue to tempt the prey within range. It is one of the few back-fanged snakes that are dangerous to people.

KEEP AWAY!

The boomslang, a tree-living snake from tropical Africa, is the most dangerous of the back-fanged snakes. A startled boomslang hisses loudly and puffs up its throat to twice its normal thickness, so that its scales stand out like bristles. This scares off most other animals.

Cobras are famous for the way in which they expand their necks when they are alarmed or angry. This usually reveals a startling mask-like pattern, with one or two

VENOM CONTROL

SNAKE venom is produced and stored in specialised salivary glands in the roof of the mouth. The poisonous components of the freshly made venom are packed into tiny globules surrounded by fine membranes. The poison itself is not released from these packets until the venom is pumped out, so the snake is in no danger of poisoning itself. Vipers can control the amount of venom they release. They usually inject smaller amounts of venom into their enemies than into their prey because they don't need to kill their enemies – just deter them. Sometimes vipers bite without injecting venom at all. Some, like this Sumatran pit viper, may simply frighten their enemies away.

FANGS

VENOMOUS snakes belong to three main groups: vipers, back-fanged snakes, cobras and their relatives. Vipers have long fangs at the front of their mouths. The fangs are folded back when the mouth it shut, but swing forward ready to strike when the snake opens its mouth. This hog-nosed viper (left) is ready to strike. Back-fanged snakes generally have small fangs at the back of the mouth and usually feed on small animals. Few can open their mouths wide enough to sink their fangs into large creatures. The third group includes mambas, which have fairly short fangs at the front of their mouths but can inject their venom into their victims much more easily than back-fanged snakes. Coral snakes and cobras also belong to this group.

eye-like markings. The pattern warns animals that might tread on the cobra by accident. The snake appears even more frightening because of the way it rears its head and moves its head round to face any disturbance.

Green mambas are related to cobras. They are the slimmest of all the really poisonous snakes. The black mamba lives mainly on the ground and is the fastest of all poisonous snakes. It can probably reach 25 km/h in a short dash, although it is normally much slower. It can slide along with its head raised about 50 cm above the ground. Mambas feed mainly on lizards, birds and small rodents.

▲ The gaboon viper has the longest fangs of any snake. They are about 2 cm long. The snake is hard to spot on the forest floor and hisses when large animals approach.

◄ The Indian cobra rears its hood in threat or fear.

✸ BLUFFING IT OUT ✸

PRETENDING TO be much bigger or fiercer than you really are is a good way of frightening your enemies and making sure that they do not press home an attack. Many harmless animals deceive their enemies by displaying this kind of frightening behaviour whenever they are disturbed. Displaying large eye-like markings is a particularly good form of bluff, especially when the markings are revealed suddenly. Many moths raise their front wings when they are disturbed, and reveal large eye-spots on their hindwings. These eye-spots look like the eyes of much bigger animals, such as cats or owls. Several bush-crickets and bugs behave in a similar fashion, and so do some mantises.

FALSE HEADS AND FALSE FACES

Many caterpillars have eye-like markings near the front of their bodies. These spots are generally quite small when the

▼ **This hawkmoth caterpillar from Malaysia hangs upside down and frightens attackers by lunging at them. The** markings near the front of its body look like eyes and the whole insect looks like a snake.

PLAYING DEAD
. . . .

SOME animals pretend to be dead when they are disturbed. They become rigid and often fall to the ground and become motionless. In the rainforests a variety of snakes, stick insects and some butterflies and moths do this. As long as they remain absolutely still, they are usually quite safe because most predators are interested only in moving prey. It would take a sharp-eyed predator to see two moths amongst these dead leaves.

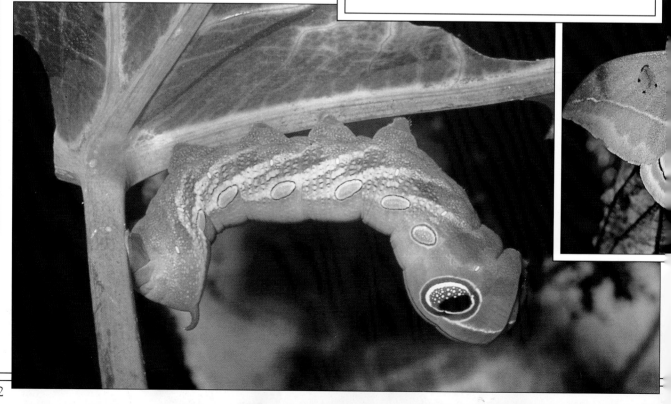

A NUMBER of butterflies and other insects have dark spots or other patterns at the rear of their wings. These can easily be mistaken for the insects' heads. Many of them also have thread-like outgrowths that resemble antennae. Birds and other predators are often fooled by these insects and they attack the wrong end. Instead of getting a nice juicy mouthful, all they get is a bit of a false antenna or wing as the insect flies off in the opposite direction. Can you make out which is the front- and which the back-end of this butterfly?

▼ When this silkmoth (centre) is startled it opens its wings to reveal huge eye-spots that deter attackers.

▼ When this leaf-litter frog (bottom) is alarmed it turns away from the disturbance and shows two large eye-spots on its rump, transforming it into a frightening face.

caterpillars are feeding or resting, but when a caterpillar is disturbed it puffs up its front end and the eye-spots swell up like the markings on a balloon. The caterpillar may also lift its front end and move it from side to side. Birds and other predators mistake it for a snake and keep well away.

SOUNDS TERRIFYING!

Some mantises bluff their way out of trouble with the aid of sounds. When a mantis is alarmed it raises its wings and then brushes its abdomen against them. The wings are quite stiff and the action produces a rustling or hissing sound. Many birds and other small animals seem to be frightened of hissing sounds and they back away, although the mantis is not really dangerous. The insect may add to its warning by displaying bright colours or eye-spots. Several other insects, including various caterpillars and cockroaches, make hissing noises when touched.

ESCAPING from enemies and avoiding being eaten is an important part of life for most animals. Some of them, particularly animals that live in open country, rely on speed to get away from their enemies. Others are protected by spines or other weapons, and many others are poisonous. Others simply pretend to be poisonous or dangerous, and some even pretend to be dead. But most small animals escape the attentions of their enemies by using some form of camouflage. This kind of trickery uses colours and patterns to conceal the animals so that their enemies do not notice them.

Camouflage is particularly well developed in the rainforests, where huge numbers of animals are trying to find food and even more are trying to hide. The rainforest animals have evolved some really amazing survival tricks.

BLENDING IN

The simplest way of hiding is to blend in with the surroundings, and this is exactly what many insects and other small creatures do. Many caterpillars have exactly the same green colour as the leaves on which they feed and they are very difficult to see.

Glasswing butterflies use a different method to blend in with their backgrounds. Their wings are almost completely transparent, so you can see the leaves or flowers behind them without even noticing the butterflies. Bark mantises can wait for their prey on tree trunks without being seen, and so can various geckoes and other lizards.

▶ The shape and colour of this moth make it indistinguishable from a broken twig – so long as it stays absolutely still.

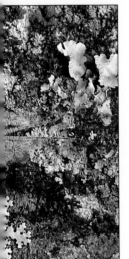

Guess what!

Can you make out the creatures in these pictures? They may look like bits of plants but all of them are insects.

They are:
1. a bark mantis
2. two prominent moths
3. a stick insect
4. a lichen katydid
5. a praying mantis
6. an orion butterfly.

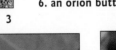

1 2

3 4

5 6

BREAKING UP OUTLINES

Larger animals also benefit from camouflage. Most deer and antelopes have a dark back and a paler underside, an arrangement known as countershading. The pale underside counteracts the shadows and helps the animal to blend in with its background more easily.

The leopard's spotted coat looks like patches of light and shade and helps to camouflage the animal in the forest. The leopard has no real enemies, but camouflage helps it to creep up on its prey without being seen. The tiger's stripes do the same thing by breaking up the outline of its body. The zigzag patterns of many snakes also help them to hide from their prey on the forest floor.

Patterns that break up an animal's outline are called disruptive patterns. They usually consist of two or more colours with sharp dividing lines between them. Predators' eyes are drawn to these boundaries and they do not notice the shape of the whole animal. Many moths rely on these patterns to break up their outlines when resting on tree trunks and other surfaces.

▲ A katydid from the South American rainforest is perfectly disguised as a shiny green leaf.

▼ The Asian horned frog is more likely to be trodden on than spotted on the forest floor.

▲ Perched on a branch, the potoo looks more like a gnarled stump than a bird.

▼ Transparent wings make this glasswing butterfly almost invisible.

LOOKING LIKE TWIGS AND LEAVES

Birds and other predators do not eat twigs or leaves and so they take no notice of insects that resemble them. Many caterpillars are extremely twig-like, and often bear little bumps that resemble buds. Some stick insects are even more twig-like. The insects nibble leaves at night and usually spend the daytime clinging to twigs. They even sway gently from time to time, as if being blown by the breeze. Their skins are often the same colour as the twigs and this makes the insects very difficult for predators to see.

Leaf insects, which live only in Southeast Asia, are closely related to stick insects, but their bodies are amazingly flat and leaf-like. Flaps on their legs look like pieces of nibbled leaves. Bush-crickets also include some remarkably leaf-like species. The veins on their wings match those on the surrounding leaves, and the wings often bear pale spots that resemble the natural blemishes on the leaves. This form of camouflage, in which animals resemble twigs and leaves or other objects in their surroundings, is called protective resemblance.

Looking Like Flowers

Mantises are gangly insects that lurk among the rainforest trees. Most are green or brown and are well camouflaged among the leaves and twigs. Unless they are exceptionally hungry, mantises lie in wait for prey to come within reach of their spiky legs. Their prey is rarely aware of the danger. Other mantises are quite colourful, and these are more likely to be found in flowers. Some look so like flowers themselves that insects come to drink their nectar and find themselves being eaten instead.

Colour-Changers

Chameleons prowl slowly and almost unseen through the forest. These lizards are masters of camouflage, for they can change their colours to match various backgrounds. Their bodies are flattened from side to side and often look quite leaf-like. They even sway on the twigs as if fluttering in the breeze.

Blue and yellow layers in the skin combine to give most chameleons an overall green colour, but the animals can change this by altering the distribution of a black pigment. This pigment is contained in little packets with branches spreading through the surface layers of the skin. If the pigment is pumped into the branches, the skin becomes darker, and if the process continues the chameleon becomes

▲ This butterfly met its death in the claws of the flower mantis, which it did not see lurking in the flowers.

▼ The diamond pattern on this snake's skin breaks up its outline so that other animals cannot see its complete form.

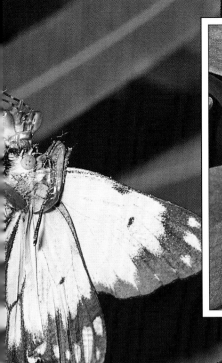

almost black. If the pigment is drawn back into the packets, the skin surface becomes pale. The colour change takes just a few minutes and can produce almost all shades of yellow, green and brown.

As well as changing colour to match different backgrounds, chameleons can change colour according to their moods. When they are frightened, many species become almost black, and this probably frightens their enemies. Some chameleons also puff themselves up with air when they are frightened. This makes them appear bigger and more frightening to predators.

▲ This orchid mantis (right) from Malaysia looks as inviting to visiting insects as the flower on which it sits, perfectly disguised.

▼ Like chameleons, anoles can swiftly change their colour. This one's skin is just like the branch on which it sits. Its colourful throat pouch is enlarged when it is excited or alarmed.

✹ GLOSSARY ✹

Amazon The great river in South America and the area around it, which contains the world's largest rainforest.

Bacteria Microscopic forms of life that play an important role in the breakdown and recycling of dead plants and animals. Many of them, often known as germs, cause disease in living plants and animals.

Bush-crickets Insects like grasshoppers, but with long antennae, that live in bushes and other undergrowth.

Camouflage Skin colours and patterns that help an animal blend with its surroundings and avoid the attention of predators.

Cocoon A silken bag that many caterpillars spin around themselves before turning into pupae, or chrysalises.

Countershading A form of camouflage in which the underside of an animal is paler than its back, counteracting the shadows underneath and helping the animal to fade into the background.

Disruptive pattern Any kind of pattern that breaks up an animal's outline and makes it more difficult to see. It usually consists of bold stripes or blotches.

Edible Good to eat.

Equator An imaginary line around the centre of the earth mid-way between the north and south poles.

Evolution The process by which plants and animals slowly change from generation to generation, gradually giving rise to new species that are adapted to different habitats and different ways of life.

Fang Name given to any large tooth, but especially one that can inject poison.

Gland Any organ in the body that produces and releases substances for action either inside or outside the body. Digestive glands make juices to digest food, while venom glands produce poison to attack other animals.

Herbivore An animal that feeds only on plants.

Ichneumons Insects related to wasps that lay their eggs in the eggs or larvae of other insects, so that their offspring have fresh food when they emerge.

Katydids Various kinds of bush-crickets, especially in America. Many of them have evolved remarkable camouflage.

Leaf insects Insects that are related to stick insects and resemble leaves.

Liana A climbing plant with long, woody stems that hang from the trees like ropes. Also known as lianes or vines, lianas belong to many different plant families.

Mantis Member of a group of predatory insects related to cockroaches. Mantids have long spiny front legs.

Mimic An animal species that gets some protection or other benefit by resembling another species – called the model.

Mimicry A form of trickery in which a harmless or edible animal avoids being eaten because it looks like a harmful or inedible creature.

Mimicry ring A group of animals, not necessarily related, that benefit by sharing a similar pattern of warning colours.

Model A venomous or otherwise harmful species with warning coloration that is copied by other species, known as mimics.

Natural selection The weeding out of weak and inefficient individuals during the process of evolution. Because the weakest ones are removed in each generation – usually by predators – the population as a whole gets stronger and more efficient.

Osmeterium A fleshy scent gland possessed by various caterpillars. It is blown up just behind the head when the caterpillar is alarmed and it frightens predators.

Paralyse To cause paralysis.

Paralysis Inability to move, sometimes brought about by poison.

Predator Any animal that hunts and kills other animals for food.

Prehensile tail A tail that can grip a support by wrapping around it.

Prey Any animal that is killed by another animal for food.

ENDANGERED!

●●●●●●●●●●●●●●●●●●●●●●●●●●●●●●●●●●●●

RAINFORESTS are vitally important to the well-being of the world but they are in danger of destruction. Many of the animals and plants featured in this book are under threat from forest clearance. If you are interested in knowing more about rainforests and in helping to conserve them, you may find these addresses and websites useful.

Friends of the Earth, Rainforest Campaign, 26-28 Underwood Street, London N1 7JQ

Rainforest Foundation, A5 City Cloisters, 188-96 Old St, London EC1V 9FR

Worldwide Fund for Nature
WWF (Australia), Level 5, 725 George Street, Sydney, NSW 2000
WWF (South Africa), 116 Dorp Street, Stellenbosch 7600
WWF (UK), Panda House, Weyside Park, Cattershall Lane, Godalming, Surrey GU17 1XR

Worldwide Fund for Nature
http://www.wwf-uk.org

Friends of the Earth
http://www.foe.co.uk

Environmental Education Network
http://envirolink.org.enviroed/

Rainforest Foundation
http://rainforestfoundationuk.org

Rainforest Preservation Foundation
http://www.flash.net/~rpf/

Survival International
http://www.survival.org.uk

Sustainable Development
http://iisd1.iisd.ca/

Rainforest Action Network
http://www.igc.apc.org/ran/intro.html

◀ The map shows the location of the world's main rainforest areas.

Protective resemblance A form of camouflage in which an animal resembles a leaf or a twig, or some other object in which predators have no interest.

Pupa The stage in an insect's life during which it changes from a larva or caterpillar into an adult.

Rodent Any mammal belonging to the order Rodentia, which contains rats and mice, squirrels, and guinea pigs. Most of them are purely planteaters and all have sharp, chisel-shaped front teeth.

Salivary glands The glands in an animal's mouth that secrete saliva. The main function of saliva is to start the digestion of food. Snake venom is a special kind of saliva.

Secretion Substance produced and released by a gland.

Stick insect Slender insect that resembles a plant stem or twig.

Sting Sharp pointed structure at the end of the body, through which insects, such as bees and wasps, inject venom to paralyse prey and defend themselves. Scorpions also have stings.

Tropics Hot or warm regions that lie between two imaginary lines, also called tropics, north and south of the equator.

Venom A poison that is fired at or injected into prey or an enemy.

Venomous Having venom, used for defence or to kill prey.

Warm-blooded Warm-blooded animals keep their bodies at a constant high temperature, no matter what the surrounding temperature may be. Birds and mammals are warm-blooded animals. Amphibians and reptiles are cold-blooded.

Warning coloration Bold or bright skin colours or patterns that warn predators that an animal is poisonous or has other unpleasant features.

✺ INDEX ✺